Dizzy in a Room of Fragile Things

Deimos Finley

BookLeaf
Publishing

India | USA | UK

Presentation by *BookLeaf Publishing*

Web: www.bookleafpub.com

E-mail: info@bookleafpub.com

ISBN: 9789363314887

First edition 2024

*For my boys, Malachi and Aster. The loves
of my life, and my biggest cheerleaders.
And cookie, the cat, my little stinky
princess.*

ACKNOWLEDGEMENT

To Mali, my cover artist and my lifetime

PREFACE

I can't promise that this little book is going to make much sense.
But for the weird ones, for the ones in pain, for the confused and the concerned.

For someone, anyone out there.

Journal of the Side Character

I wrote this when I was a teenager, no more than 16. I was in high school at the time, fighting my depression with little help from therapists or medication. It was an interesting time in my life, to say the least. It seems a good a place as any to start this off.

Talking to someone is like reading a book. Their expressions form the indentations in every paragraph. Every subject is like a chapter, and the paralyzing anxiety overcomes me as I realize I'm nearing the end.
It's horrifying as I stare across my boyfriend's loving features. He speaks with such a forced interest that it's only a matter of time before the page tears. His words were marked like the paper cut from chapter eight when the characters were fighting so much that you were overly eager to see who won.

He whispers about just wanting to be alone, with his computer. With his games and maybe a bit of lotion.

Mental note, do laundry. No more clean socks.
This chapter is shorter than the rest, but only
because it contains so little interest.
Like my life at home, without him.

First-person experience is always the most cruel.
The anxiety and the fear that makes me
overthink every word I say and every step I take
marks a word, an indent in the page. There are
so many of them, just as if I were to be living in
a poem. But it's a sad one, with a looming
suicidal tone.

All parts of a book, of a sentence never made
sense to me. I couldn't tell you what a verb is,
but I can go on about the chapter in my life
when I risked my entire internet existence on
pranks. I couldn't give you an example of an
adjective as well as I could tell you about when I
stopped believing in god and became an atheist.
I couldn't give you a noun, but I could tell you
how my mother's eyebrows turn red when she's
trying not to cry, how she sleeps when she's
avoiding anything.

I could tell almost every chapter in my life.
Maybe the one where I spent an entire summer
in Shodair, a children's mental hospital?

Or about the week I almost got arrested for
stealing?
Maybe I could talk about the months when I
spent all of my time lying in bed, listening to my
alarm, and wondering if life was worth the effort
of living.

I start a lot of my chapters like that. This must
be one of those sad books. The ones that make
you angry at the side characters, the ones who
hurt and beat the main protagonist.
Or make you upset at the main character for not
seeing something the author decided to let you
see.
It hurts a lot. I'm constantly feeling like a side
character.

My presence is often forgotten when I'm in
public. The people I call friends don't notice
when I cry in the back or shudder with distaste
at the stubborn and constant drama. They don't
see when I hang back, let everyone walk on, and
forget while I walk alone.
And I'd like to keep it that way. I'd rather be
alone than be forgotten, interrupted while
speaking, and never given the chance to finish.

This is my book. The side characters book.
Maybe I'll be the abrupt death, the suicide

towards the end of the story for the rest of the
cast to have a development with.
Maybe it'll be the death in the middle where it
causes a string of drama, the entire plot hill.

Maybe I'll be the wise old woman at the end,
giving advice that changes the plot, or the old
man brandishing a sword that turns the fight.
 Maybe I'll turn into something big, turn into the
main character.
But for now, I'll stay a side character. After all,
someone's gotta be in the binding, holding
everything together, right?

Outside

I was doing another challenge, self imposed at one point and told myself to write about being outside, something that I loved. I was a teen at the time, still having no trouble at all seeing the beauty in the natural world.

I love being outside. Outside at night, with the wind blowing just enough to feel the chill.
I love being outside at night, having the ability to look up at the sky and see that the stars are shining and that the trees are swaying in the wind. I can hear the crickets chirping, and the cars from the highway.
I feel the concrete beneath me, and the wind caressing my cheeks. I listen to the bugs singing their insane song and look at the stars and the light off in the distance.
 I feel so at home, with my super-sized sweater and my baggy pajama pants. The music of being outside in here is pure darkness, and feeling ungodly happy. Is this where I belong?

Yes.

Loss

I was prompted to write about something that I
don't usually write about. It took a while to think
about it, and I figured that loss is such an
opposite to love, yet fits right together like a
puzzle piece

Something so common and so hard
Hurting down to the core
Yet confusing and difficult concept to grasp
Loss so big that it tears you apart from the inside
Wandering, searching for what once was
Hoping that it'll come back
Hoping that it'll fill the hole that it left
Wishing
Wishing loss away

I miss you

Character Correlation

An impromptu poem about characters and how they relate to us, their makers. I was doodling at work one slow evening and was stricken with inspiration.

I've got a character named Scary Williams
A poor boy with haunted eyes and thin arms,
Piercings and scars to boot
He's a wonderful example of how writers tend to
put themselves in the shoes of their creations
He hurts like I do, haunted by old memories and
bullies only he knows of
But he fights harder than I do,
Throwing Molotov cocktails at his suppressors,
and waving flags in the face of danger
Fighting for his right to be who he his
Fighting for his presence in this world

He is much more than I could ever be,
Yet is so much more of me than my hands
A perfect example
Of who I want to be

"Clouded and Curious"

When I was a preteen, I was obsessed with Alice
and Wonderland dynamics. It was honestly, kind
of cringe, but I wrote putting myself in the
position of the Cheshire cat, with my boyfriend
at the time being the Mad Hatter. That in of itself
is a long story, but I wrote some interesting
things within my life. Here's an excerpt!

My mind is crowded with the fog of a drug,
Slit pupils crossing.
And I want to do something...
But that sober thought keeps hitting the train-

Go to sleep, Go to sleep,   Go to sleep.

But my sketchbook calls to me with the quill and
it's pewter,
The bath and it's steaming water,
The squeak of the chew toys...

Go to sleep,   Go to sleep,   Go to sleep!

Sugar spikes in my blood,
The warmth accepts me.

May be, it is best if I,
Go to sleep, Go to sleep,   go to sleep.

"Coins"

Another excerpt from my journal from an odd
perspective of a young Cheshire Cat, this poem
centers around money, a common trouble of
most everyone.

Coins are the foundation of living.
Three for this, five for that.
The round, gold circles do everything.
Why?
Why can't we pay in leaves.
So much easier to do.
Leaves are plentiful.
Dip them in copper if you must.
But leaves should be the new currency.
It matters not whether you want to
Save our forests or

Precious metals

Wishing Well

This one is on the sadder side of the spectrum, a vent poem from several years ago now. This breakup was the worst that I've had so far, and it brought out many difficult emotions that I sprawled out onto a page.

I wish that I could have let you in. I wish I could have kept you.
But instead, my dreams, my fantasies pulled me away.
Hopefully, we will meet again. In another life, with another love. But instead it should be.
You can come to me and grasp my hand with vigor and hope.
And just as you pull me into embrace, you have to push me away. As hard as you can, shove me to the floor and tell me that it will never happen.
Break my heart the way I broke yours.
Tear it out of my chest and burn it.
Tear it to shreds.

And just as I am able to whisper, 'But I love
you."
You tell me,
"No. You just love the idea of me."
'It will never happen. You hoped for nothing.'
And you will shut me down.
You will break me, just as I broke you.

Daisies

This poem is much more recent. One of my partners, Mali, had been giving me small and enjoyable tasks to do in a day as enrichment. I believe the task was simply, "Write something." This is what came of it.

Daisies are such pure flowers,
Usually white, or pastel in color.
A sign of innocence, childhood
Purity all in the form of a flower.

Rings of daises, flower crowns
Pure, unbridled imagination
Curable by worry and doubt
By adulthood slowly taking hold of our thoughts

The ones once overwhelmed by...
What flower was it?
Oh yeah, daisies!
I had those in my yard when I was a kid.

03/21/2019

This is another skit from that rough breakup when I was a teenager. Again, it brought tons of interesting and negative emotions that live in my files, on pages. This one didn't have a title, but was signed and dated.

Maybe I'll understand one of these days why the
real me wasn't enough for you
And the world will start spinning again at
normal speed
And I'll be able to watch the sunset
Without worrying
About leaving your wretched
Beautiful face behind

Battlefields

This poem was found in an old journal of mine. It's not dated anywhere in the book, but is filled out with many different vents of a life I don't remember. I've felt a lot of pain, most of which I'm not too sure where came from. But as I keep saying, pain can bring out some beautiful and interesting things.

I don't know where to turn
I see so blurred without help
I don't know where to go because all I see is
darkness
The setting sun and the rising moon

As I pour out my soul onto what will soon be
In many years to come
A faded page

A wasted soldier bleeding out as the war rages
on
Watching his friends fall to the nightmare
infested bullets of enemy fire

A darkness only I see
Only me
I am me, I see what I see when no one else does
The sound of graphite against a page
A burned love letter that will never reach it's
destination

A dying soldier who's only wish is to come
home
A teenage girl
Who fears pain but wants nothing but to hurt
A sleeping figure with a screaming shadow
I am that soldier
That paper, that letter
That girl
A broken soul
A shattered heart

A grain of sand in the beach of life
Just another casualty
To breathe away
In the brink of time

Want

I'm struggling with a few desperate and intimate
emotions, and have had these thoughts rolling
around in my head for a few days. Enjoy!

Why don't you want me?
I don't know what I'm doing wrong.
I'll change for you.
I'd become anything that you want.
Is it my hair?
I'll cut it all off.
Is it my nails?
I'll bite every single one of these acrylics off.
Am I too feminine?
I'll burn my skirts and my makeup.
Am I too masculine?
I'll become the girl of your dreams

I'd revert everything I've ever
Burned late nights away
I'd throw out every little piece I had of myself

Id give away all the parts of me that make me
who I am
I would dispose of my heart
Just to hear those words from you
Just to feel like I was the one you wanted

Do I try too hard?
I won't care at all
I'll ignore you
I'll hide the excitement when you kiss me
Roll my eyes when you say you love me
I worry that I do anyway
Even when you

Tell me you love me
Kiss me
Hold me
You don't seem like you want it
Why do you love me to make me go away?
Why don't you want me?

Memories

Another impromptu poem, a thought that has been rolling around in my mind for a few days now.

I collect so many things, you could probably call me a hoarder.
I hate throwing away glass, proven by the box of bottles out in the garage.
I love knicknacks, my shelves filled with sculpted music boxes and ceramic frogs.
I adore the idea of reading, thus my shelves are full of novels.
I despise empty walls, so plain white pain is covered in paper and canvas and tapestry.

I also collect unseen things.
I collect hurt, and history.
I collect knowledge like a dryer filter collects layers and layers of pet hair.
But most important of all...
I collect memories.

Like the time in 7th grade when I had to help my
budding best friend with a beading project in
history class.
I don't remember exactly what birthday it was,
but I received a pink digital camera, and there
was a gummy bear beach cake, with swimming
friends enjoying a day in the sun.
I remember playing the drum set in church
before everyone else arrived for the service, and
the pastor encouraging me to do so. Playing
loudly in an echoing chapel, playing for no one
but myself.
I remember the first time I really felt connected
with my partner. I don't remember what was said
before, something illegal suggested, followed by
a whisper to my Chromebook, "For legal
reasons, that was a joke." He laughed so hard
that he almost fell out of his chair, in the middle
of high school history class.

I am akin to a faded, trashed photo album,
hidden in the bottom of the storage unit. Some
of the sleeves are torn, scratched and covered in
a mysterious goo. Some of the pictures are
smudged and blurry, the image in question
beyond repair.
Some of the images bleed in light, a rainbow
crossing over someone's face.

Eyes shining bright in the sun.
Grinning faces, smiling memories.

I collect experiences
And I've never been good at taking pictures.

Mine

Stop looking at me like I have the world in my
eyes if you want me to pay attention -M

How am I to stop
Looking at you
When you are my world
My heart
My life
I want to cry when I think of the world without
you
Without your joy
Without your ridiculousness
I wouldn't be able to stand a world without you
So I sit here
With stars in my eyes
Tears in my heart
All for you
My world
The world in my eyes

Trees

Another journal entry that I've found incredibly interesting.

A tree.
I want to be a tree.
A tree feels no pain ?

A leaning oak, to home his friends.

A thick redwood, to stand above all.

A hulled birchbark, to stay standing strong.

A whispering willow.
To whisper secrets to you.
Singing into the wind and drinking by the river.
I want to be a tree. But I know my pain would
dry my leaves.
Would snap my branches.
Would scar my bark.

I want to be kind.
I want to stand tall.

I want to be strong.

But my unheard secrets still spill
Through my singing, swaying branches

Aster

Something sweet about one of my boyfriends.

He's like an icy winter day.
Eyes are pucks of ice, dribbling water every time
Melting at things that he loves.
His lashes are a dark sand color, fanning the
melting ice
He's so cold yet winter is a warming season
Cuddled under blankets, drinking cocoa next to
a blazing fire
Skin is rough like an unpolished crystal,
Soft, work worn hands that send shivers through
my spine like the dribble of cold water rolling
down my back
A man that changed everything I knew
Who helps me sleep days away
Under warm blankets
Next to a blazing fire
Radiating comfort
Radiating peace
Not a care in the world

Mali

And more sweetness, for my other boyfriend.

My home
A world without you is a world without air
I miss you even when you're next to me

How could I breathe without your hand around
my heart?
Squeezing it and
Keeping it beating
I love your soft hands and
Razor sharp nails
Skin still soft as flower petals

I could say so many things
Call you so many ethereal things
But not a one could ever speak
How you make my heart ache when you cry
Soar when you laugh

Goddess that I acutely worship
Grant me your light
Never leave my mind

Allow me
To be your follower
Forever

"Me n You"

I thought that I was running out of old material when I remembered that I have a habit of writing love letters. To loosely quote the recipients, "I imagine that these will be found in the far future by someplace like a museum."

People think that love is like an arrow or a cannon ball.
But when you're as oblivious and insecure as I am, it's more like a poison dipped blade.
The wound will heal because the blade is short, but the poison will spread.

It first gets into your blood.
To your heart, making it beat faster.
Then it goes to your throat, tightening and making it hard to speak.
Then your skin, making it wet with nerves and eagerness.
Finally, steeping into your brain, then you'll know what it's like,

To be struck with that poisoned blade
Pierced with the heart tipped arrow
Blown away with the love-soaked cannon ball
It hurts but feels so God damn good

To remember that I am loved so dearly
That someone so sickly sweet, so easy to ramble
to
So beautiful
It's sad
Could love someone like me
Who's a broken vase pieced back together with
gold and copper

Rain

I'm still hunting for old material and new inspiration. On my hunt for things to add, I found some old songs that I never fully turned into music. This one in particular was the product of a story I was writing with someone, and our characters were very much in love. I think I might revisit the thought of writing music again.

Stay with me until the rain pours
I'll spin you around,
And kiss you
And love you until the end of time
So just let me love you in the way I do
And I'll spin my world around my arms
Tell him that in no way would I ever want to replace him

And I want to make it rain for years just to kiss him
In the rain
So let me love you,

Kiss you,
Breathe in your love

And I just wish to list
All that I see,
So let me whisper what I hear and taste
What I see of you
Stay with me until the rain pours,
I'll spin you around,
And kiss you,
And love you until the end of time
So just let me love you in the way
I do
And I want to make it rain for years just to kiss
him
In the rain
And maybe He'll say yes
If I ask him to marry me

Paint

This was another song that never got produced. It was long and required quite a bit of editing to be turned into the poetry it was meant to be. A lot of people agree that music is poetry in its own way, and I couldn't agree more.

You bleed out your watercolor
Your streak lies on my skin
Skin-colored canvas…

And as I look over at my skin
At the gentle dots of color
Melted into my flesh
I'll ask you to

Paint on me, cry your tears
Bleed all your lies onto my skin
With the magnum strength acrylic you use
Airbrush your broken words onto my thighs
And splatter lies onto my back with that fanned brush

Suck on that thick, expired yellow watercolor as
you stroke your ego
I wish I could see what your problem is
Get the hell out of my business
Lick the paint off your fingers
I don't have the time for this
You don't have anything to use against me

But I will watch you work with a passion
I envy
Watch ME work, baby
And kiss your canvas goodbye

Sing your bleeding song
Cut through cut thighs
Paint the painted canvas

Cover your hands in that permanent ink and let
yourself fall into the depths of the palate
Paint on my body
Cry out your tears

Feel free to bleed your bloody shades, but make
sure to save some for your next canvas
Paint on me, cry your tears bleed your lies onto
my skin like the magnum-strength acrylic
Brush your crying words onto my bleeding
thighs and splatter your lies across my back

Suck on that yellow watercolor but save that paint
For the next canvas

Forget

Another song that I was trying to build a tune for on my guitar way back when I was teaching myself guitar. This came from that old relationship I keep mentioning. I was a lot more involved in my craft back then.

I wanna forget
I wanna forget your lips
Your words
Your teeth and your smile
Your praise, your love

Every time I think of you, the gaping hole
Where my heart s'posed to be
Opens up again

I thought I buried you
Burned you
Threw you in the trash
I thought I ditched you
Tossed you into the ashes

Please let me forget
The way you said I love you
The way you said goodbye

Maybe there's a reason I should cry

Maybe if I showed you
How broken you made me
Maybe if I saw you again

Just let me forget
Just let me forget
Just forget the way your hair hung
Forget The way you smiled
Forget The way you said hello
Forget the way you shined

Maybe I can dream that you're still mine
I can't believe you're gone
Maybe it is for the better

I'll see you in my dreams, my love, farewell
See you in my paradise, maybe then you'll be
able to show me
We weren't meant to be

Just because I have someone new doesn't mean
you're not here with me
Doesn't mean I'm right to move on like that

I got someone new
Maybe now I'll forget
Forget that it was you